Detaining and Deporting Undocumented Immigrants

Other titles in the *Immigration Issues* series include:
Birthright Citizenship
Border Control and the Wall
The Dreamers and DACA
Refugees and Asylum

Detaining and Deporting Undocumented Immigrants

John Allen

ReferencePoint
Press®

San Diego, CA

For more information, contact:
ReferencePoint Press, Inc.
PO Box 27779
San Diego, CA 92198
www.ReferencePointPress.com

LIBRARY OF CONGRESS CATALOGING-IN-PUBLICATION DATA

Name: Allen, John, 1957– author.
Title: Detaining and Deporting Undocumented Immigrants/By John Allen.
Description: San Diego, CA: ReferencePoint Press, [2020] | Series: Immigration Issues | Includes bibliographical references and index. | Audience: Grades 10–12
Identifiers: LCCN 2019034569 (print) | LCCN 2019034570 (ebook) | ISBN 9781682827833 (library binding) | ISBN 9781682827840 (ebook)
Subjects: LCSH: Illegal aliens—United States—Juvenile literature. | Illegal aliens—Government policy—United States—Juvenile literature. | United States—Emigration and immigration—Government policy—Juvenile literature.
Classification: LCC JV6483 .A436 2020 (print) | LCC JV6483 (ebook) | DDC 364.1/370973—dc23
LC record available at https://lccn.loc.gov/2019034569
LC ebook record available at https://lccn.loc.gov/2019034570

Contents

An Ongoing Immigration Crisis

In late May 2019 US Customs and Border Protection (CBP) agents had a problem on their hands. A flu outbreak at the holding facility in McAllen, Texas, on the border with Mexico, threatened the hundreds of undocumented immigrants held inside. Just days before, a teenage Guatemalan boy had fallen sick and died at a nearby holding station. With more than thirty migrants showing signs of flu, and thousands more arriving every day, CBP officials decided to close the McAllen center for a day. Agents set about scrubbing and sterilizing the facility from top to bottom. Migrants in detention were moved from the "freezer"—their term for the frigid air-conditioned center—to chain-link enclosures outside. Many of them, though poor, had never experienced such conditions. "Thank God we're OK," said Carmen Juarez, who had journeyed a thousand miles on foot from Chiquimula, Guatemala, with her six-year-old daughter. "We slept on the hard ground, under the stars. No mattresses, just a silver blanket. My daughter had a fever and that's why they asked us to sleep outside."[1] A CBP nurse made sure that Juarez's little girl received treatment at a local hospital. It was a typical day in the Rio Grande valley, which has become ground zero in the ongoing immigration crisis.

No Easy Solutions

The crisis at the southern border has been years in the making. Despite changes in policies and programs, both President George W. Bush and President Barack Obama struggled to stanch the flow of undocumented immigrants into the United States. A major reason that Donald Trump won his surprising victory in the 2016 presidential election was his promise to address the problem of illegal immigration. During his campaign, Trump declared he would build a wall to keep out those intent on crossing the border illegally. He also promised to round up and deport undocumented people who were already living in the United States. Trump often characterized the undocumented as criminals and gang members, claiming they were involved in smuggling illicit drugs and committing violent acts. His opponents accused him of exaggerating the problem and appealing to racial prejudice to stir up anger. They insisted that the vast majority of undocumented immigrants came to America in search of steady work and a better life.

The issue came to a head in May 2018 when the Trump administration announced a new "zero tolerance" policy toward undocumented immigrants. The policy drew angry reactions nationwide as migrant families were separated at the border, with their children held in fenced enclosures or shipped to facilities miles away. Border patrol agents stepped up efforts to arrest migrants who had failed to show up for hearings on their status or had entered the country illegally. In the ensuing months, migrants continued to flood across the border. Caravans of asylum seekers from Central America only added to the problem. (The US government may grant asylum, or refugee status, to immigrants who are escaping persecution or violence in their own countries. Those granted asylum can work in the United States and eventually apply for citizenship.) Detention facilities in border cities and towns could not handle the influx. In late June 2019, after months of failure to compromise, Congress finally passed a $4.6 billion bill aimed at easing the overcrowding in detention centers and providing care for migrant families and unaccompanied children.

The nation remains divided on the issue of detention and deportation of undocumented immigrants. Most Americans recognize that there are no easy solutions to the problem. A January 2019 *Washington Post*/ABC News poll found that 54 percent of the American public believes the United States is not doing enough to keep undocumented immigrants from entering the country. Yet a February 2019 Gallup poll found that more than eight in ten would allow immigrants currently in the country illegally to become citizens should they meet certain requirements. On the question of deporting undocumented immigrants, the public is narrowly split. In a March 2019 Pew Research Center poll, 46 percent favored deportation and 47 percent were opposed.

Balancing Enforcement and Immigrant Rights

Trump supporters want US laws about illegal entry to be vigorously enforced. In June 2018 Trump himself tweeted, "We cannot allow all of these people to invade our country. When somebody comes in, we must immediately, with no Judges or Court Cases, bring them back from where they came."[2] However, contrary to Trump's words, undocumented immigrants do have many rights under the US Constitution once they are on US soil. The Bill of Rights refers to "people," not "citizens." Thus, the Fourteenth Amendment's assurance of due process—the right to a fair trial or court hearing—also applies to undocumented immigrants. Those seeking asylum have the right to a hearing regardless of their legal status. Most other migrants are granted a hearing before an immigration judge to determine their status. In July 2019 the Trump administration launched a fast-track deportation plan that called for migrants who have been in the country illegally for less than two years to be deported almost immediately. Migrants who return to the United States despite a previous order of deportation can also be removed at once.

"We cannot allow all of these people to invade our country. When somebody comes in, we must immediately, with no Judges or Court Cases, bring them back from where they came."[2]

—Donald Trump in a June 2018 tweet

Men are crowded into an immigrant detention center in McAllen, Texas, in 2019. Conditions in the center became so unsanitary that the entire facility had to be decontaminated.

With the recent flood of undocumented entries, the legal process has been overwhelmed. The raw numbers are staggering. Border agents arrested 268,044 migrants in the five months from October 2018 to February 2019, twice the number from the same period the year before. As many as 76,000 migrants entered in February 2019 alone. The year 2018 saw 162,000 asylum claims submitted at the southern border, while 250,000 undocumented immigrants were deported.

The vast majority of migrants arriving today are families from Central America. Most request asylum at the border, seeking to escape poverty and violence in their own countries. This explosion has raised many issues related to detention and deportation, including family separations at the border and overcrowded and unhealthy conditions at detention centers. Underlying this crisis is a struggle to balance enforcement with protection of immigrant rights. "The system is well beyond capacity, and remains at the breaking point," says Kevin K. McAleenan, commissioner of the CBP. "This is clearly both a border security and a humanitarian crisis."[3]

Chapter One

Family Separations at the Border

"When will I see my papá?"[4] Five-year-old José asked that question repeatedly in his native Spanish upon arriving in Michigan in May 2018. His only possessions were a trash bag filled with dirty clothes and two stick-figure drawings, one of his family in Honduras, the other of his father. He last saw his father at the US border in El Paso, Texas, being led away by border patrol agents. Their perilous trek north from Honduras across Mexico had come to a wrenching end. José's father was taken into custody for illegally entering the United States, and José, separated from his dad, was flown hundreds of miles away to live with a foster family.

According to Janice, José's foster mother in Michigan, the child cried miserably for the first several nights. He refused to change clothes or be touched or hugged. His only comfort was the crumpled drawings of his family he kept under his pillow. Like thousands of migrant children from Central America, José found himself in a bewildering situation due to Trump's aggressive—and controversial—policy toward undocumented immigrants. Janice and her family have cared for other underage refugees in the past several years. However, this was the first time a child had been left with no way to contact a parent. "I'm watching history happen before my eyes," said Janice. "It's horrendous."[5]

A Tough New Policy

Upon taking office, Trump set about keeping his campaign promise to fix the problem of illegal crossings at the southern border. One proposed solution was to build a wall or other barrier to keep migrants out. Another idea was to separate migrant parents from their children at the border. Trump and his advisers believed such a policy would demonstrate a new, tougher approach to the problem and act as a deterrent to other migrants seeking to enter the country illegally. In March 2017 former general John Kelly, then serving as secretary of the US Department of Homeland Security (DHS), revealed that talks about separation had taken place. Kelly later said families would be separated only if the child's life was in danger.

From July to October 2017, the DHS quietly tested a family separation program in and around El Paso, Texas. Any adult who crossed the border illegally in the so-called El Paso sector, extending from West Texas to New Mexico, was arrested and prosecuted. Those who arrived with young children had to relinquish them into the hands of border officials while the adults awaited a hearing. "This was happening in El Paso before it was news," says Linda Rivas, executive director of Las Americas Immigrant Advocacy Center. "People didn't believe it."[6] A DHS official confirmed that the family separation program was in use.

In April 2018 the Trump administration went public with its tough new stance on immigration at the southwestern border. The aggressive new policy was called zero tolerance. In his announcement of the change, Attorney General Jeff Sessions made it clear that family members would be separated once they were in custody. "If you are smuggling a child then we will prosecute you, and that child will be separated from you as required by law," Sessions declared. "If you don't like that, then don't smuggle children over our border."[7] The effort

"If you are smuggling a child then we will prosecute you, and that child will be separated from you as required by law. If you don't like that, then don't smuggle children over our border."[7]

—Attorney General Jeff Sessions

revved up quickly, with twenty-three hundred children separated from their parents in little more than a month. The Office of Refugee Resettlement, an agency within the DHS, scrambled to find housing for the detained children. For example, many were sent to a converted Walmart or to warehouses near the Texas border, while preschool-age children and toddlers were taken to so-called tender-age shelters in the Rio Grande valley. Some migrant children ended up thousands of miles away in foster-care facilities in East Harlem, New York.

The frequent chaos inside the Trump administration affected the rollout of its zero tolerance effort. As investigators from the Government Accountability Office (GAO) discovered months later, the new policy caught many agencies unprepared. Among these were the DHS and the US Department of Health and Hu-

A father from Honduras becomes emotional after being separated from his children at the border between Texas and Mexico. The Trump administration's zero tolerance immigration policy resulted in thousands of children being taken from their parents and detained separately.

man Services (HHS). Agency officials had no plans ready to handle the thousands of children who were taken from their parents. Often, when these children were transferred to shelters, the shelter staff were not notified of their situation. They learned the children had been separated from their parents only when the children told them. Some children were held in fenced enclosures at warehouses or military bases. As New Jersey representative Frank Pallone Jr. observed, "This disturbing GAO report shows the tragic consequences of carrying out a cruel and misguided policy impacting thousands of families without any preparation or prior notification to the agencies charged."[8]

"This disturbing GAO report shows the tragic consequences of carrying out a cruel and misguided policy impacting thousands of families without any preparation or prior notification to the agencies charged."[8]

—New Jersey representative Frank Pallone Jr.

Outrage over Family Separations

The Trump administration was caught off guard by the national reaction to its zero tolerance policy. People of all political persuasions expressed shock and outrage. There were newspaper stories of wailing toddlers being pulled from their parents' arms. Cable news shows broadcast images of children languishing in fenced enclosures—or cages, as critics called them. (Later reports acknowledged that the Barack Obama administration had also held migrant children in caged areas with concrete floors.) Liberal pundits demanded an end to the policy, calling it not only cruel but incompetent. Democrats in Congress reacted with anger and decried the fact that such things could happen in America.

Congressional Democrats were not the only ones to speak out against separating children from their parents. Many Republicans, including veteran senators Orrin Hatch and Lamar Alexander, also urged Trump to abandon the new policy. Foreign leaders such as British prime minister Theresa May and French president Emmanuel Macron questioned the wisdom of the separations. Even First Lady Melania Trump and Trump's daughter Ivanka publicly voiced their misgivings. Advocates for migrants insisted the family separation program was illegal. They contended that it treated all immigrants at the southwestern border as criminals, even those with legitimate asylum claims. Moreover, it sought to solve the border crisis by punishing innocent children.

Faced with mounting political pressure, Trump backtracked on family separations. On June 20, 2018, he issued an executive order aimed at keeping migrant parents and children together indefinitely while their legal cases moved through the courts. Trump made it clear, however, that the change would not end enforcement at the border. "We're going to have strong—very strong—borders," Trump said while signing the order in the Oval Office, "but we are going to keep the families together. I didn't like the sight or the feeling of families being separated."[9] Critics noted that Trump's order did not end the zero tolerance policy, and they raised alarms that families might be crowded together in inadequate facilities such as tents or makeshift cages. The order also said nothing about reuniting the twenty-three hundred children who had already been separated from their parents.

Democrats and the media also stressed how Trump's hardline immigration policies were affecting real people. One detainee, thirty-nine-year-old Marco Antonio Muñoz, ended up committing suicide in his detention cell. Muñoz had been separated from his wife and three-year-old son at the border and had no idea where they were or whether he would see them again. Virginia senator Tim Kaine blamed Trump's policy for Muñoz's death. "So as we try to reassemble 2,300 families that this administration has spread to the winds, there will be at least one 3-year-old boy

"The Dreamers have a sympathetic case. There are circumstances under which I and others would be happy to support that. But we need to do more than that. You know there's some genuine fixes on the legal immigration side and on the illegal immigration side that need to be addressed."[44]

—Mitch McConnell, Senate majority leader

Americans Oppose Family Separations

A large percentage of Americans did not support the Trump administration's practice of separating migrant children from their parents. This is revealed in the University of Maryland Critical Issues Poll conducted in March–April 2019. Poll results additionally show that most Americans want the US government to keep families together even if this leads to fewer criminal prosecutions.

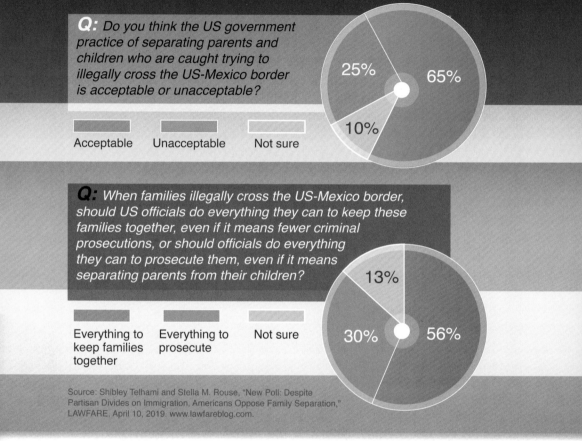

Q: Do you think the US government practice of separating parents and children who are caught trying to illegally cross the US-Mexico border is acceptable or unacceptable?

25%   65%

10%

Acceptable   Unacceptable   Not sure

Q: When families illegally cross the US-Mexico border, should US officials do everything they can to keep these families together, even if it means fewer criminal prosecutions, or should officials do everything they can to prosecute them, even if it means separating parents from their children?

13%

30%   56%

Everything to keep families together   Everything to prosecute   Not sure

Source: Shibley Telhami and Stella M. Rouse, "New Poll: Despite Partisan Divides on Immigration, Americans Oppose Family Separation," LAWFARE, April 10, 2019. www.lawfareblog.com.

who will not be able to reunite with his father," Kaine said. "I ask this president, I ask the attorney general, I ask the secretary of Homeland Security, was it worth it? Was it worth it?"[10]

The Courts and "Catch and Release"

Six days after Trump's reversal, a federal judge in San Diego ordered a halt to family separations at the border. Parents could be separated from their children only if they were known to have a prior criminal record or were somehow unfit to have custody. In his

Despite Court Order, Family Separations Continue

In June 2018, with tensions rising across the United States over the border crisis, a federal judge in California ordered the federal government to halt most family separations and reunite migrant children with their parents. Soon afterward, Trump issued an executive order that supposedly ended the policy of separating migrant families at the border. Yet one year later, immigration advocates were pointing out that little had changed. Hundreds of children were still being wrenched from the arms of their parents and transported hundreds of miles away to live in foster homes or child care facilities.

In a court filing at the end of July 2019, the American Civil Liberties Union (ACLU) claimed that more than nine hundred migrant children had been taken from their families in the past year despite the policy change. According to the ACLU's filing, the Trump administration was relying on dubious charges of criminal behavior or abuse by migrant parents in order to seize their children. The DHS has a legitimate interest in separating migrant children from parents who are guilty of serious crimes or are physically abusive. Yet the ACLU found that parents with minor traffic offenses or drug possession charges were being forced to relinquish their children. "When [family separations] happened under prior administrations there were usually strong indicators of real and legitimate child welfare concerns," says Lisa Coop, associate director of legal services for the National Immigrant Justice Center. "What we're seeing right now is of an entirely different character. These are gratuitous separations."

Quoted in Lomi Kriel and Dug Begley, "Trump Administration Still Separating Hundreds of Migrant Children at the Border Through Often Questionable Claims of Danger," *Houston Chronicle*, June 22, 2019. www.houstonchronicle.com.

ruling, Judge Dana Sabraw offered scathing criticism of the Trump administration's policy. He said there was no system to track children after they were separated from their parents, enable children to communicate with parents, or reunite parents and children after legal proceedings. Sabraw ordered officials to reunite all parents with minor children under age five within fourteen days and with minor children age five and older within thirty days. In effect, he ruled that the family separation policy violated the due process rights of migrants—both adults and children. Federal judges in other states also moved to stop the separations.

Legal rulings against the zero tolerance policy referred back to the Flores agreement of 1997. Under this agreement, the federal government cannot detain unaccompanied migrant children under age eighteen for more than twenty days. Thus, after twenty days children have to be released. In 2014 the Flores agreement was triggered—and actually expanded—due to actions by the Obama administration. To deal with an influx of migrant families, Obama's DHS built a number of family detention centers to hold both adults and children. After immigration lawyers sued to have the children released under the Flores agreement, the courts decided that Flores pertained not only to children but to entire families of migrants. This ruling led Obama's DHS to release many undocumented immigrant families into border communities. Obama administration officials considered separating migrant parents from their children in order to hold the adults legally but rejected the idea.

Many conservatives, including Trump, contend that the Flores agreement makes it almost impossible to control illegal immigration. If families must be kept together and can only be held for twenty days, then after that period has elapsed, they must be released. Although migrants are required to return for hearings on their legal status, conservatives claim that many families simply ignore the orders and fade into the border towns. Trump and his supporters refer to this situation as "catch and release." They argue that it actually encourages migrant parents to bring their children across the southern border illegally, secure in the knowledge they will be released in a short time. Trump repeatedly blames this "loophole" on his predecessor.

In May 2019 the US Department of Justice's Executive Office for Immigration Review reported that 44 percent of migrants released from detention in 2018 did not show up for their immigration court hearings. This is half the rate of no-shows that Vice President Mike Pence claimed in a June 2019 interview on CNN. It is also far more than the 2 percent to 10 percent failure-to-appear rate that immigration advocates claim. These statistics remain a bitter point of contention between the two sides of the immigration debate.

Like Obama, Trump has struggled to stop the flow of illegal entries at the border while still abiding by Flores. As Nicholas Wu, a reporter on immigration issues, explains,

> The Flores Agreement plays a large role in the Trump administration's implementation of its "zero-tolerance" policy and the resulting family separations. The Trump administration tried to get around Flores by taking children away from their parents, thereby allowing their parents to be held indefinitely, while their children were housed separately.[11]

A frustrated Trump desperately wants to get the Flores agreement reversed, or at least revised. Congress could do it, but the Democrat-led House is opposed. Another option is for the US Department of Justice to draft new regulations that would effectively nullify Flores. In August 2019, the Trump administration announced new rules that would enable the detaining of undocumented children and their parents indefinitely. This would do away with the twenty-day limit under Flores. However, the new regulations were being challenged in federal court.

Reuniting Migrant Families

The task of reuniting migrant families, as ordered by federal courts, has proved to be difficult. To start, the government had to compile a complete list of families that were affected. Adding to the difficulty, an unknown number were separated in the months before the policy officially went into effect. "No one but a few in the government knew that these separations had been going on nine or 10 months before, and that hundreds if

> "No one but a few in the government knew that these separations had been going on nine or 10 months before, and that hundreds if not thousands of children were [being separated]."[12]
>
> —Federal judge Dana Sabraw

After being separated for more than a month, an immigrant mother and daughter are overjoyed to be reunited in Houston, Texas. As of April 2019, several thousand children were either back with their families or placed with friends or relatives.

not thousands of children were [being separated]," said Sabraw. "The court didn't know that and plaintiffs didn't know that, and I don't think government counsel knew that."[12] In an April 2019 court filing, the government said it could take up to two years to identify all the migrant children who were separated at the border.

Trump officials at the HHS also noted that many migrant children had been living in sponsors' homes or child care facilities for months. They argued that removing them now and reuniting them with parents awaiting court dates would be traumatic for the children. Groups like the ACLU blasted this argument, saying the Trump administration simply did not want to make the effort to reunite families.

One factor adding to the difficulty of reuniting families is the lack of an effective tracking system for migrant children. Once the children were released at the border, the Office of Refugee Resettlement lost track of them. To manually review the cases of nearly fifty thousand children—the estimated number of migrant children released to relatives, foster families, or some other sponsor since July 1, 2017—would swamp the resources of the refugee office. Instead, the office has used computer statistical analysis to match children with their parents.

Red Tape and Raw Emotion

As of April 2019 about twenty-eight hundred children had been returned to their families or placed somewhere approved by their parents (for example, with friends or relatives). Each story has its own measure of bureaucratic red tape and raw emotion. Seven-year-old Angie and her father, Adelino, came to the United States seeking asylum due to threats of violence in their native Honduras. On June 1, 2018, border officials in McAllen, Texas, seized the sleeping Angie from Adelino, who was raising the child by himself. Angie was sent to Houston and the home of her mother, whom she barely knew. Meanwhile, Adelino was transported to a Southern California holding facility. Adelino feared that his request to get Angie back would result in the child being put in detention.

A migrant-rights group called Immigrant Families Together learned of Adelino's case and offered to help. The group negotiated the red tape of the immigration system and secured his release by paying an $8,000 bond. Adelino flew to Houston, where Angie, accompanied by reporters and news cameras, was waiting at the airport. When a beaming Angie ran into her father's arms, it ended a separation that had lasted 326 days. Adelino admitted he had been almost crazy with worry during those long months in detention. He could scarcely imagine what his child was going through.

The Trump administration's decision to separate migrant children from their parents at the southwestern border has drawn fire from the start. The policy has led to migrant parents being held in custody with no idea where their children are. It has landed migrant children in foster homes and child care facilities far from the border. Reactions to the policy in the United States and around the world has been overwhelmingly negative. Court orders to

The Flores Agreement

The Flores agreement was a legal settlement designed to improve detention conditions for unaccompanied minors who enter the United States illegally. It is named for a fifteen-year-old girl from El Salvador named Jenny Lisette Flores. In 1987 Flores and three other Central American children filed a class action lawsuit, *Flores v. Reno*, against the US government. The suit claimed that the Immigration and Naturalization Service (INS) had held the children in conditions that were unacceptable for minors. It took ten years, but the government finally reached an agreement with the plaintiffs. The agreement sets out the proper standards of care for detention of minors:

> Following arrest, the INS shall hold minors in facilities that are safe and sanitary and that are consistent with the INS's concern for the particular vulnerability of minors. Facilities will provide access to toilets and sinks, drinking water and food as appropriate, medical assistance if the minor is in need of emergency services, adequate temperature control and ventilation, adequate supervision to protect minors from others, and contact with family members who were arrested with the minor.

> The INS was reorganized, renamed, and placed under the DHS in 2003, but the DHS also must abide by the terms of the Flores agreement. Since 2015 US district court judge Dolly Gee has cited the government several times for not providing safe and sanitary living conditions for migrant detainees. For example, in 2019 the DHS was ordered to provide soap, toothbrushes, and other items for basic hygiene.

Quoted in Camilo Montoya-Galvez, "Here's Why the Trump Administration Says It's Not Required to Give Migrant Children Soap," CBS News, June 24, 2019. www.cbsnews.com.

end the separations and reunite migrant children with their parents have only begun to improve the situation. Meanwhile, many Trump supporters worry that new protections for migrant families, while intended as humane, will actually encourage more parents from Central America to bring their children on the perilous journey to the US border.

Chapter Two

Health and Safety Issues at Detention Centers

On July 2, 2019, the DHS's Office of Inspector General issued an alarming report about conditions in detention centers in the Rio Grande valley. The report warned of dangerous overcrowding and overextended stays for migrants in custody. Photos showed women and children sleeping on mats on the floor with nothing but flimsy Mylar blankets for warmth. One holding cell designed for forty-one occupants was stuffed with eighty-eight male adults. Some enclosures were so crowded that those inside were forced to stand for hours or even days at a time. Detainees sometimes tried to clog toilets with socks or towels so that they could escape their cells for a couple of hours while maintenance was performed. Emblematic of the dire situation was a cardboard sign in the hand of one detainee saying only HELP. Officials at the DHS blame the strained conditions on the recent surge of migrant families from Central America. With its resources, both human and material, severely overtaxed from the influx, the agency has struggled to cope with the crisis. And thousands more migrants are arriving each week. As the DHS admitted in a public statement, "The current migration flow and the resulting humanitarian crisis are rapidly overwhelming the ability of the Federal Government to respond."[13]

Outrage at Detainees' Conditions

The report by the DHS inspector general was met with public outrage and calls for change. Democrats blamed Trump's policies for the chaos at detention centers. Several Democratic lawmakers, including members of the Congressional Hispanic Caucus such as New York's Alexandria Ocasio-Cortez and Texas's Joaquin Castro, traveled to the border to view conditions for themselves. Certain members livestreamed their visits to packed detention centers. They pointed to problems with water and sanitation in the centers and claimed that detainees lacked simple items such as soap, shampoo, toothbrushes, and combs. They passed along reports of children crammed into facilities with nowhere to sleep. They described detainees banging on windows and pointing to their beards to indicate how long they had been in custody. Some in Congress called for widespread firings at the DHS.

Other Democrats, while sympathetic to the challenges of dealing with a flood of undocumented immigrants, still found the situation unacceptable. "I strongly believe in border security, and I believe that our immigration system is broken and requires a major overhaul," said Elissa Slotkin, a first-term representative from Michigan. "But let me be clear: There is no rationale that excuses how our government is treating the migrants, in particular the migrant children."[14]

Outrage over the detention centers extended beyond the shores of the United States. In early July 2019, Michelle Bachelet, the United Nations High Commissioner for Human Rights, issued a scathing assessment of the situation. Bachelet declared that she was appalled by the conditions migrants and refugees were subjected to on the southern US border. She called for the widespread release of detainees. Bachelet described how migrants and refugees were seeking protection from violence and hunger. But instead, she said, "when they finally believe they have arrived in safety, they may find themselves separated from their loved ones and locked in undignified conditions. This should never happen anywhere."[15]

"When they finally believe they have arrived in safety, they may find themselves separated from their loved ones and locked in undignified conditions. This should never happen anywhere."[15]

—Michelle Bachelet, the United Nations High Commissioner for Human Rights

Hundreds of immigrant children, mostly from Central America, are shown in a holding cell. They are sleeping with only flimsy Mylar blankets for warmth.

Characteristically, Trump took issue with the critics and blamed Democrats for not addressing "loopholes" in asylum laws to ease the overcrowding in detention centers. He noted that border patrol agents in these facilities were so swamped that they had to do things they were not trained for, including medical work and janitorial service. Trump countered the DHS inspector general's report with praise for the detention centers he had visited. "I've seen some of those places, and they are run beautifully," he said. "They're clean. They're good. They do a great job."[16]

An Aid Package for Detention Centers

Despite Trump's positive spin on the facts, officials in his administration have stressed the need for more money for detention centers. The HHS is a good example. The HHS's job is to run the shelter system for migrant children and find appropriate sponsors, such as foster parents and private child care facilities, to care for the children. However, HHS officials contend that their facilities are already beyond capacity. Therefore, the length of time incoming migrant children must remain in border patrol custody continues to grow, a situation that is bad for the children and frustrating for the border patrol. Lack of funding also has led to cuts in recreational and educational programs and legal aid in HHS shelters. Children languish there, crowded together with nothing to do.

In June 2019 administration officials told Congress that funding to maintain detention centers was due to run out at the end of the month. With daily media reports focusing on the dire conditions at the border, Congress resumed a bitter debate on a $4.6 billion aid package. Some Democrats in the House wanted tight

Making Millions Running Shelters for Migrant Children

Many detention centers and shelters in the United States are run by private companies. In Texas, the epicenter of the immigration crisis, contractors operate more than thirty facilities. Sixteen other states have a total of more than one hundred shelters that are privately run. Winning a government contract to house, transport, and care for migrant children can be a lucrative prize for a business. It can mean hundreds of millions of dollars in government payments over several years.

Shelters are set up in former schools, stores, and medical centers. One of the largest private shelters in the country is a former Walmart in Brownsville, Texas. Known as Casa Padre, the facility now houses as many as fifteen hundred migrant boys in custody of the Office of Refugee Resettlement. Most of the boys either came to the United States unaccompanied or were separated from their parents at the border. The shelter is run by Southwest Key Programs, a nonprofit that was paid more than $450 million in fiscal year 2018 to operate shelters for migrant children. Immigrant support groups generally give Southwest Key passing grades for its shelters. Most of its employees speak Spanish, and many receive training to help them deal with children whose parents are missing or in custody miles away. Yet even Southwest Key has been criticized for understaffing its shelters to cut costs. As one former employee notes about the company's hiring practices, "You could say, 'Oh I babysit my sister' and they'd hire you."

Quoted in Kavitha Surana and Robert Faturechi, "Here's What It's Like to Work at a Shelter for Immigrant Kids," ProPublica, June 27, 2018. www.propublica.org.

restrictions on how the money would be spent. They worried that pouring money into expanding a detention system that was already dysfunctional would solve nothing. Some even favored dismantling the detention system altogether so that migrant children could no longer be held in overcrowded facilities. In general, many Trump opponents did not trust the administration to use the aid package to help make conditions better for detainees. "Expanding detention centers means more people are going to be detained and that puts more people at risk," said Clara Long, senior researcher at Human Rights Watch, "when the best way to ensure that children are safe and that asylum seekers' rights are respected is to opt to release people and have them live in communities and with their families."[17]

In the end, however, Speaker of the House Nancy Pelosi pushed through a compromise with the Republican-led Senate, and the funding bill passed. Republicans and Democrats alike hoped that the aid package would enable migrant children held by the border patrol to be transferred more quickly to HHS shelters. Democrats insisted on tougher requirements for standards of care at short-term detention centers. They also established a rule that children could be kept in the centers no longer than ninety days.

As for Republicans and Trump supporters, they hoped that the funding bill was the beginning of what they believe is a more rational response to the border crisis. Some Republicans in Congress blasted Democrats like Ocasio-Cortez who had compared the detention centers to concentration camps. They pointed out that Hispanic migrants were not trying to escape the United States, they were trying to get in and take advantage of the nation's security and prosperity. "[Ocasio-Cortez] says that the men and women of our border patrol and our authorities are intentionally running concentration camps on the southern border," said Republican senator John Neely Kennedy of Louisiana. "She needs to go to the Holocaust Museum and see what a concentration camp is."[18]

Dealing with Disease and Abuse

There are more than two hundred DHS detention facilities operating in the United States, most in isolated locales far from major cities. The DHS spends more on immigration enforcement and detention than on all other federal criminal law enforcement efforts combined. With the recent influx of migrants at the southern border, detention centers are strained to the breaking point. Due to overcrowding, centers struggle to provide sufficient medical care and sanitary conditions for detainees. For example, in May and June 2019, border patrol facilities located close to the southwestern border held from fourteen thousand to eighteen thousand detainees each night. Human rights groups complain that the detention centers are often run like jails or prisons. They believe the centers should instead be operated as humane shelters, which is more in keeping with what they claim is the misdemeanor level of most migrants' legal status.

As the immigration crisis has grown worse, media reports have focused on the ongoing chaos at federal detention centers.

Children peer through fencing in an area where they are detained in McAllen, Texas. Often, these children have little to do all day because there is no funding for educational or recreational programs.

They have documented unsanitary conditions due to overcrowding, as well as breakouts of infectious disease, including mumps, chicken pox, flu, pneumonia, tuberculosis, cholera, and typhus. Medical workers have no idea about the vaccination history of migrant children. They warn that not only are the detainees at risk, there is also the increased hazard of outbreaks in the wider community. Border personnel who come in contact with the mi-

Undocumented Immigrants in Prison

Opponents of the Trump administration's immigration policies often compare detention facilities to prisons. However, thousands of undocumented immigrants who have been convicted of crimes are being held in actual prisons in ten states. These facilities are privately run and contain both citizen and noncitizen prisoners. According to the US Sentencing Commission, about one-third of all people sentenced to prison each year in America are illegal immigrants. These prisoners are due to be deported immediately after they complete their sentences. Inside prison walls, they are held separately from nonimmigrant prisoners and receive different treatment as well. Critics say the Federal Bureau of Prisons, which runs these facilities, discriminates against undocumented inmates by denying them benefits and services available to other prisoners.

The Federal Bureau of Prisons claims it has a mission to provide offenders with opportunities for work and self-improvement. It seeks to help inmates become law-abiding citizens. Yet none of this seems to apply to undocumented prisoners. They are almost always denied access to drug counseling and job training programs that are available to inmates who are citizens. Part of the problem lies with the private corporations the government hires to run the prisons. Critics say rehabilitation of prisoners is not a priority when the goal is to make a profit. As investigative reporter Jonathan Blitzer observes, "The logic appeared to be that, because these inmates would eventually be deported, the government need not expend additional resources on them."

Jonathan Blitzer, "A New Study Uncovers Troubling Information About Immigrant-Only Prisons," *New Yorker*, March 13, 2019. www.newyorker.com.

grants are especially at risk—both of contracting illnesses and of spreading them to the wider population.

There have also been complaints of physical, verbal, and sexual abuse at detention centers. In February 2019 the US Department of Justice revealed that in the previous four years it had received more than forty-five hundred complaints from undocumented immigrant children about sexual abuse while in detention. The children were stranded in the United States, either having entered the United States alone or somehow being separated from their parents on the journey north from Mexico or Central America. Federal officials claim that most cases of abuse involve employees of private contractors, not government personnel. But such a distinction makes little difference to the victims. "Simply because these children may have entered the country illegally doesn't mean they forfeit their rights to being treated with dignity and respect," says Lyndon Haviland, former chief executive officer of Darkness to Light, a group committed to the prevention of child sexual abuse. "And it certainly doesn't entitle those entrusted with their protection the right to commit unspeakable crimes against helpless minors under their care and supervision."[19] Immigrant rights groups emphasize that the federal government has a legal responsibility to protect migrant children from abuse. And the Flores agreement mandates that children be housed in conditions that are safe and sanitary.

> "Simply because these children may have entered the country illegally doesn't mean they forfeit their rights to being treated with dignity and respect."[19]
>
> —Lyndon Haviland, former chief executive officer of Darkness to Light

A Facility Under Fire

One facility that has drawn intense scrutiny during the immigration crisis is in Clint, Texas, a farm town of about nine hundred residents in El Paso County. Located just 4 miles (6.4 km) from the border, the Clint detention facility is a large compound set off from surrounding fields and pastureland by a fence of razor wire. Buses of migrant children arrive and depart from the Clint center at irregular intervals, along with supply trucks and border patrol vehicles. Details about day-to-day operations at the facility are generally not publicized, so few people in town know exactly what goes on behind the gates.

In late June 2019 a team of immigration lawyers, doctors, and interpreters visited the Clint detention center to check for its compliance with the Flores agreement. The team discovered that increasing numbers of children were being sent to the Clint facility even though it had previously been reserved for adult migrants. On the day the team did its inspection, there were about 350 children in the facility, most from Guatemala, El Salvador, and Honduras. The numbers were constantly changing as busy border patrol officials received new arrivals and transferred others to an Office of Refugee Resettlement site. Nonetheless, for a center with a capacity of 104, the team found obvious problems of overcrowding. To handle the overflow, guards at the Clint center had moved many children into a large warehouse out back, keeping them in rooms with no windows. Some children said they had been held in the Clint facility for more than three weeks, and they were still awaiting processing.

According to the team, conditions at the Clint center were appalling. Babies lacked diapers, and the children's clothing stank of sweat and urine. With a shortage of cots, children were forced to sleep on the concrete floor. Most had only a single wool blanket and had to decide whether to use it as a mattress on the hard floor or as a blanket for warmth in the frigid air-conditioning. The investigating team also found very young children consigned to the care of older children. Guards would hold up a two-year-old or three-year-old and ask for someone to take care of the child. When the older children got bored, they would hand the toddlers off to someone else. Some toddlers were left abandoned and crying on the floor.

On the last day of the team's visit, officials at the facility discovered a lice infestation. Children with head lice were sharing combs and brushes, which only spread the infestation. According to the observers, border patrol agents punished a small girl who had lost her brush by making her sleep on the floor instead of on a cot. The facility also experienced an outbreak of flu, with one sick girl quarantined in a separate room. Five infants in the facility were judged by the team's pediatrician to need immediate treatment in the town's neonatal intensive care unit.

The team's report on the Clint facility expressed the members' shock and dismay at what they observed. The team's attorneys wrote:

> Children are held for weeks in deplorable conditions, without access to soap, clean water, showers, clean clothing, toilets, toothbrushes, adequate nutrition or adequate sleep. The children, including infants and expectant mothers, are dirty, cold, hungry and sleep-deprived. Because the facilities deny basic hygiene to the children, the flu is spreading among detained class members, who also are not receiving essential medical assessments or prompt medical treatment.[20]

Warren Binford, the woman who leads the clinical law program at Willamette University in Oregon, said she had never seen conditions so bad, calling them prison-like. The immigration lawyers hoped to obtain inspections at all CBP facilities in the Rio Grande valley and El Paso areas. They also planned to seek a court order finding the federal government in contempt of court for violations of the Flores agreement.

"The children, including infants and expectant mothers, are dirty, cold, hungry and sleep-deprived. Because the facilities deny basic hygiene to the children, the flu is spreading among detained class members."[20]

—June 2019 legal and medical team report on detention facility in Clint, Texas

US Representative Alexandria Ocasio-Cortez gives a statement to the media outside an immigrant detention facility in Clint, Texas. She and other lawmakers toured the facility in June 2019 after a report on overcrowding and poor conditions was made public.

The Face of the Immigration Crisis

All at once the Clint detention facility became the face of the immigration crisis. Newspapers and broadcast news shows passed along the team's findings about overcrowding, filth, disease, and lack of medical care, among other failings. In an attempt to respond to these reports, the DHS and the border patrol invited reporters to tour the Clint facility a week after the immigration team's visit.

Reporters observed that some of the overcrowding had been eased with stepped-up releases of migrant children. Children were seen outside shooting baskets or kicking soccer balls. Officials pointed out that workers sometimes brought toys and sports equipment for the children to play with. One border patrol agent, a seven-year veteran at the facility, admitted the children cried occasionally—not from mistreatment, but because they were homesick and missed their parents. El Paso border patrol sector chief Aaron Hull insisted the facility mostly had adequate supplies for the detainees. Hull said the children received three meals a day, including oatmeal for breakfast, ramen noodles for lunch, and a microwaved burrito for dinner. Some agents expressed hopes that visiting lawmakers would return to Washington, DC, with a renewed determination to address the detention problem.

Stung by all the attention and criticism, personnel at the Clint facility defended their efforts. They disputed the immigration team's version and claimed the team's tour had been much less extensive than the later one for reporters. The personnel emphasized the challenge of caring for small children in a facility designed for temporary detention of adults. Like many residents of Clint, Dora H. Aguirre, the town's mayor, believes the agents deserve some sympathy too. "They're just trying to do their job as a federal agency," says Aguirre. "They are trying to do the best they can."[21]

Trump's zero tolerance policy, combined with a surge of migrants at the southern border, has strained detention centers in the United States to the breaking point. Inspection reports by the DHS and by outside teams of observers have spurred outrage about inhumane conditions at the facilities. Of particular concern is the lack of adequate care for migrant children. A compromise aid package in Congress promises to help. However, humanitarian groups say the whole detention system needs to be overhauled—or eliminated. For now, Americans remain divided on the use of detention centers, just as they are on nearly every aspect of immigration policy.

"[Detention center employees are] just trying to do their job as a federal agency. They are trying to do the best they can."[21]

—Dora H. Aguirre, mayor of Clint, Texas

Chapter Three

Aggressive Deportation Efforts

Donald Trump's tweet of June 17, 2019, sent shock waves through many Hispanic communities in America. "Next week ICE will begin the process of removing the millions of illegal aliens who have illicitly found their way into the United States," Trump posted on Twitter. "They will be removed as fast as they come in."[22] Although the plan had reportedly been in the works for months, officials at the US Immigration and Customs Enforcement (ICE) seemed to be caught off guard. Details of the crackdown remained vague. Many pundits questioned whether ICE even had the budget and personnel to undertake such a massive effort. But experts on immigration law thought they could detect the true intent of Trump's announcement. "I think that these tweets really accomplish two things," said Hiroshi Motomura, an immigration law expert and professor at the University of California, Los Angeles.

> One is to play to his base. I don't think he needs to deport millions of people to convince them he is doing something. The second thing he is trying to accomplish is to make people afraid. People will leave on their own. You make them afraid so they keep their heads down and low.[23]

Sowing Fear with Deportation Threats

If Trump's deportation threats were intended to sow fear among undocumented immigrants, they succeeded. ICE officials said they would focus on individuals who had received final orders of deportation after going through due process. Even those who had settled with their families far from the border grew uneasy at the prospect of being arrested. In Highlandtown, an immigrant neighborhood in Baltimore, Maryland, many undocumented Salvadorans, Guatemalans, Hondurans, and Mexicans braced for the coming federal raids. Immigration lawyers reminded people of their constitutional rights. They advised undocumented individuals not to open their doors to agents without a warrant and not to sign any documents. Reverend Bruce Lewandowski sought to help immigrants seeking shelter and advice at his Highlandtown church. Lewandowski condemned the plan to conduct raids on neighborhood families. "I characterize it as an act of domestic terrorism," he said. "People are afraid, really afraid."[24] Immigrant rights groups warned that parents might be reluctant to seek medical help for themselves or their children for fear of being apprehended at the clinic. Even going out to shop for food and other necessities could be nerve wracking.

House Speaker Nancy Pelosi led Democrats in demanding that Trump cancel the raids. She called his deportation plans heartless and said they would rip families apart and terrorize Hispanic communities. Many of the families targeted by the raids include spouses or children who are citizens, meaning that they could be left behind to fend for themselves should a family member be deported. But not everyone viewed the plight of the undocumented so sympathetically. Those who had voted for Trump in hopes that he would get tough on illegal immigration saw the threatened ICE raids as long overdue. They urged the government to follow the rule of law and deport individuals who had been processed in court and judged to be in the United States illegally. Hardliners on immigration claimed that many of those subject to deportation had a criminal record, pending criminal charges, or a history of past removals. They hoped

"I characterize [Trump's deportation effort] as an act of domestic terrorism. People are afraid, really afraid."[24]

—Rev. Bruce Lewandowski, pastor of a church in Baltimore, Maryland that a wave of deportations might deter individuals and families in Central America from trying to gain entry in the future.

In the end Trump's threats proved to be largely an exaggeration. Shortly after his original tweet, the president postponed the raids for two weeks. Trump urged Democrats in Congress to use the delay to fix what he called loopholes in the asylum process at the southern border. When the raids finally did occur in late June, they targeted two thousand families in ten cities, not the millions Trump originally mentioned. The cities included New York, Chicago, San Francisco, and Los Angeles. According to reports in the *New York Times*, the long-dreaded weekend raids ultimately resulted in thirty-five arrests. However, a few weeks later, on August 7, 2019, hundreds of ICE agents raided seven food-processing plants in Mississippi. The raids led to the detention of 680 undocumented workers. One federal prosecutor claimed it was the largest single-state immigration roundup in US history.

On June 17, 2019, President Donald Trump tweeted that ICE would begin mass arrests and deportations of immigrants who had come to the United States illegally, which caused panic among people in Hispanic communities throughout the United States.

Prior to the planned raids, Mark Morgan, acting director of ICE, claimed that many undocumented immigrants had ignored requests to give themselves up. "So what are our options?" Morgan said. "They've had due process, they've had access to attorneys, they've had access to interpreters. Majority of them don't even show up. And then when they didn't show up, they received ordered removal in absentia. We have no choice."[25] A survey by *Politico*/Morning Consult found that 51 percent of voters support aggressive ICE raids, with 35 percent opposed.

"So what are our options? They've had due process, they've had access to attorneys, they've had access to interpreters. Majority of them don't even show up. And then when they didn't show up, they received ordered removal in absentia. We have no choice."[25]

—Mark Morgan, acting director of ICE

Mass Deportations Are Nothing New

Arrests and deportations have been on the rise due to the Trump administration's zero tolerance policies. Just days after his inauguration in January 2017, Trump told the news program *60 Minutes* that he planned to deport as many as 3 million undocumented immigrants. It took several months for the new Trump agenda to take effect at ICE and other federal immigration agencies. The deportation engine revved up in 2018 as those agencies removed more than 250,000 undocumented immigrants. By June 2019 that number had increased to 282,242, with more to come.

However, large numbers of deportations are nothing new in the United States. Despite the heightened publicity over Trump's deportation policies, his most recent predecessors in the White House actually deported or returned immigrants in larger numbers. For example, Bill Clinton removed or returned more than 12 million immigrants during his two terms. George W. Bush oversaw about 2 million removals and 8.3 million returns of immigrants while in office. Removals are official deportations, in which immigrants are processed, fingerprinted, and transported to their home countries. They can then be charged with a felony should they reenter the country illegally. Returns are when migrants are

A Modest Dream

Esteban and Maria are a living example of how Trump's deportation efforts are affecting real lives. Esteban came to the United States from Central America with a modest dream of finding work and buying a few necessities. Arrested for illegal entry not far from the border, he spent a month in federal custody before he was released on bail. However, instead of waiting for his immigration hearing, Esteban rashly jumped bail and took a bus to Manhattan. He left behind a deportation order for his removal.

In New York Esteban met Maria, who had come from Colombia and was applying for asylum in the United States. She had two children from a previous marriage. Esteban and Maria got married and made plans to open a beauty parlor and nail salon business with their savings. Then one day federal agents appeared on their doorstep. Despite his clean record since arriving in New York, Esteban was subject to removal due to his failure to appear at the border hearing. He soon found himself on a plane back to Central America. Meanwhile, Maria, pregnant and nearly penniless, sought help from her church and friends to pay her rent. It took several months, but Esteban eventually made a perilous journey back to the United States to reunite with Maria and meet his newborn son. Should Esteban be arrested again, he could be banned from the country for twenty years. However, his young son is safe. Born on US soil, he is an American citizen.

simply loaded onto buses and shipped back across the border with little or no legal action.

Under Barack Obama, the DHS decided to focus more on official deportations. The number of deportations averaged nearly 400,000 a year from 2009 to 2013, with a high of 409,849 in fiscal year 2012. Only in Obama's last two years in office did deportations fall below 250,000 annually. Over its eight years, the Obama administration deported nearly 2.5 million immigrants. Due to these figures, defenders of immigrant rights labeled Obama the "deporter-in-chief." Removing immigrants who were in the United States illegally was a priority during most of Obama's presidency. For example, in a 2014 interview with ABC News, Obama addressed the influx of unaccompanied minors that were crossing the border: "That is our direct message to the families in Central America: Do not send your children to the borders. If they do make it, they'll get sent back. More importantly, they might not make it."[26]

Two Different Approaches

Although both Obama and Trump have presided over plenty of deportations, there are significant differences in how each of them approached the problem. Under Obama, ICE agents began to focus on undocumented immigrants with criminal records, including convictions for drug running or sex trafficking, and those who had only recently crossed the border. Obama decided that undocumented immigrants who were already settled in the United States and were raising families should not be a priority for law enforcement. He also believed these immigrants should be granted a path to citizenship. That is a major reason the number of deportations decreased in Obama's final two years. "If you're not targeting and focused on people who recently arrived, then the border is effectively open," says Cecilia Muñoz, a former Obama advisor who is now with the New America Foundation. "It is more humane to be removing people who have been here two weeks than it is to be removing people who have been here for 20 years and have families."[27] Obama also sought to protect undocumented young people who had been brought to the United States as children. Polls at the time showed a majority of Americans agreed with these changes in policy.

Trump, however, has made no such distinctions. For him, any immigrant found to be in the country illegally should be arrested and then deported as quickly as possible. That includes those who have otherwise obeyed laws and established lives in the United States. In 2017, Trump's first year in office, ICE agents arrested forty-six thousand undocumented individuals with no criminal records. This was an increase of 171 percent from the previous year. Many of the immigrants who have been deported under Trump had become settled members of their communities. Some had been living in the United States for decades. A number of them had indeed been issued final orders of removal. Yet they had been checking in regularly with local immigration officials—sometimes for years—and considered their status to be safe. They were the sort of immigrants Obama increasingly chose to leave alone.

By contrast, many in Trump's immigration team insist such individuals are lawbreakers by definition. Under the law, they say, there is no difference between an individual who has been in the United States illegally for ten years or ten days. According to Muñoz, it is this lack of priorities in the Trump approach that is disrupting immigrant communities. "People are in terror. They're scared of sending their children to school. That is a very, very different dynamic," she says. "There are no enforcement priorities in the Trump administration. That's the point. In the Obama administration there were clear priorities."[28] However, conservatives worry that going easy on longtime offenders is like granting them amnesty. They warn this will only encourage more illegal entries. The question of whether these people deserve special treatment goes to the heart of the immigration controversy.

Deporting Criminals

One group that the Trump administration has prioritized for deportation is convicted criminals. This is an effort by Trump to keep one of his earliest and most frequently repeated campaign promises. During the campaign he claimed that Mexico and other Latin American nations were sending their criminals across the southern US border. According to Trump, these included rapists, drug peddlers, and sex traffickers. He vowed that as president he would see to it that undocumented immigrants who had committed crimes were arrested and deported. Shortly after his election in November 2016, Trump

"There are no enforcement priorities in the Trump administration. That's the point. In the Obama administration there were clear priorities."[28]

—Cecilia Muñoz, a former Obama advisor now with the New America Foundation

On August 7, 2019, US immigration officials raided several food processing plants in Jackson, Mississippi, rounding up and detaining 680 undocumented workers. Shown is a group of these workers being guarded by an immigration officer.

repeated his pledge on national television. "What we are going to do is get the people that are criminal and have criminal records, gang members, drug dealers,"[29] he said. He also estimated that there were 2 million to 3 million illegal immigrants in the country with criminal convictions, numbers his critics have claimed are vastly inflated. The Migration Policy Institute estimates that the number of unauthorized immigrants who are convicted criminals is closer to 800,000.

Nonetheless, Trump has followed through on his promise. Soon after taking office, he issued an executive order that added a new category to those prioritized for deportation. These were immigrants who had been charged with a criminal offense but not yet convicted. During Trump's first one hundred days, ICE arrested more than 41,000 individuals who were known or suspected to be in the country illegally. Agents estimated that 75 percent of these had criminal records. Moreover, according to ICE officials, of the 256,000 immigrants deported in fiscal year 2018, more than 145,000 were convicted criminals. Among those removed were 5,900 known or suspected gang members. News releases from ICE during Trump's time in office show that unauthorized immigrants have been arrested, convicted, and deported for offenses such as weapons trafficking, drug smuggling, child molestation, financial crimes, and felony involuntary manslaughter.

Delays at Immigration Courts

The Trump administration's attempts to streamline the deportation process have met with limited success. Today the nation's immigration courts face huge backlogs around the country. Trump officials blame the logjam on the recent surge of asylum claims from Central American refugees. Opponents of the administration point instead to rules changes that are designed to speed up the process but actually have the opposite effect. For example, the US Department of Justice wants to allow judges on the Board of Immigration Appeals to issue summary judgments on deportation

An ICE official assists a man outside a building that houses ICE and the immigration court in Atlanta, Georgia. Although the Trump administration has attempted to streamline the deportation process, immigration courts are backlogged.

Turning Up the Heat on ICE

In July 2019 ICE agents found themselves at the center of the controversy over the Trump administration's deportation raids. A flurry of protests against the agency broke out across the nation. On July 12, 2019, a pro-immigration group called Lights for Liberty led hundreds of thousands of supporters in more than seven hundred cities and towns to protest against ICE. Many of the vigils were held outside ICE facilities. One day later, a man armed with a rifle attacked an ICE detention center in Tacoma, Washington. The man was throwing incendiary grenades at a large propane tank attached to the facility when police shot and killed him.

Calls to abolish ICE altogether have come from members of Congress, including New York representative Alexandria Ocasio-Cortez and Massachusetts senator Elizabeth Warren. Senator Kamala Harris, a California Democrat running for president, has also been critical of the agency's performance. "I think there's no question that we've got to critically re-examine ICE and its role and the way it is being administered and the work it is doing," Harris says. "And we need to probably think about starting from scratch." In response a White House tweet accused ICE's critics of supporting the movement of weapons, drugs, and captive victims across the border. A Pew Research poll shows that Americans are split in their opinions of ICE, with 44 percent viewing the agency favorably and 47 percent unfavorably.

Quoted in Daniella Diaz, "These Democrats Want to Abolish ICE," CNN, July 3, 2019. www.cnn.com.

cases without holding hearings that can stretch to several days. However, according to immigration lawyers, this raises the question of whether judges have considered all the evidence to make a reasonable ruling. This leads to more appeals and more delays. "All of these changes have reduced access to due process for immigrants, which may result in more deportations but also results in more appeals, and . . . it likely just results in more backlogs," says immigration attorney Martha Ruch. "The administration's actions have done more to disrupt, rather than 'streamline' the immigration court process."[30] More delays

"The [Trump] administration's actions have done more to disrupt, rather than 'streamline' the immigration court process."[30]

—Martha Ruch, an immigration attorney

would be disastrous, since the backlog nationwide has already swelled to almost 877,000 cases.

In Denver, Colorado, wait times for completing deportation cases average 962 days. Endless delays in Denver and elsewhere have left many unauthorized immigrants in limbo, nervously awaiting life-changing judgments on their future. One of these is forty-year-old Mauricio Basaves, who entered the United States illegally from Mexico twenty years ago. Saving money he earned clipping hedges, he managed to start a trucking firm in Denver, with eight drivers hauling freight for large retailers like Walmart and Target. He has three children, the oldest, at fifteen, a high school honors student. Yet Basaves got caught in a scam over his work permit. Years before, in order to get work authorization quickly, his lawyer had applied for asylum for Basaves long after the deadline for such an application had passed. Basaves ended up with a court order to appear for a deportation hearing. With no criminal history, he had never had a problem with the local immigration authorities. Now, due to Trump's more aggressive policies, Basaves has reason to be anxious about his family and business. And with the backlog in the courts, he could be looking at years of uncertainty.

Trump's zero tolerance immigration policy has increased deportations and spread fear through immigrant communities nationwide. Many Trump supporters favor the removal of all those living in the United States illegally, regardless of how long they have been here. Opponents prefer that ICE and other federal agencies concentrate on deporting criminals and recent arrivals, as was done in the latter years of the Obama administration. With more migrants and refugees crossing the southern border every day, disputes over deportation are sure to remain heated.

Chapter Four

The Rise of Sanctuary Cities

On a hot summer Saturday in July 2019, hundreds of people gathered in a park in Lawrence, Kansas, to petition city officials not to cooperate with federal authorities. Days prior to the rally, Trump had announced a sweeping series of raids to arrest undocumented immigrants. The protesters in Lawrence, which calls itself a "welcoming city," were showing solidarity with undocumented immigrants in their community. They were urging local police to withdraw support for federal ICE agents not only in the upcoming raids but on a permanent basis. The crowd also raised more than $1,600 to help local immigrants with legal fees, transportation, and groceries. In a state where 56 percent of voters voted for Trump, strong voices rang out in support of undocumented immigrants.

On the same day in Berkeley, California, a similar rally took place in Civic Center Park. As in Lawrence, hundreds of people showed up to protest Trump's immigration policies. Signs called for detention centers to be closed and ICE to be shut down. Some condemned the ICE raids as cruel and un-American. Berkeley mayor Jesse Arreguín and members of the city council expressed anger and frustration at what they saw as federal harassment of immigrants in California and elsewhere. "We are a proud sanctuary city," Arreguín told the crowd. "Our police [are] our police and will not cooperate in any way with any ICE enforcement action."[31] Council member Rashi Kesarwani went on to advise local immigrants about their rights in the event of a raid. Other council members announced that local churches and synagogues were offering *sanctuary*—or shelter and protection—for undocumented immigrants who might be fleeing from federal agents. For these politicians, city officials, faith leaders, and ordinary citizens, affirming their status as a sanctuary city served as a firm but peaceful protest against immigration policies they could not support in good conscience.

A Controversial Movement

Lawrence and Berkeley are just two of many cities, counties, and states enlisted in the sanctuary movement. As of April 16, 2019, there were eight states, including New York, Illinois, and California, that have declared themselves to be sanctuary states. More than three hundred other cities and counties also consider themselves to be sanctuary areas. The term *sanctuary city* has no legal status. It merely describes a jurisdiction that refuses in some way to comply with federal efforts to enforce immigration laws. Usually it means that local law officers and city officials are prohibited from assisting in federal deportation efforts. They are told not to question people about their immigration status, not to inform ICE about anyone suspected of being in the United States illegally, and not to voluntarily hand over undocumented immigrants to federal agents. Those who promote sanctuary policies like these tend to believe that undocumented immigrants have the right to stay in the United States as long as they do not commit crimes once they are here. Supporters of sanctuary cities and states also fear that using local police to enforce immigration laws will only serve to damage trust between officers and immigrant communities.

ICE agents arrest an immigrant in Los Angeles in 2017. Since the 1980s, opposition to the arrest and detention of undocumented immigrants has led to states, counties, and cities offering sanctuary to these immigrants, resulting in the term sanctuary cities.

In recent years sanctuary cities have become political flash points due to the aggressive pursuit of undocumented immigrants. Federal officials contend that sanctuary cities are breaking federal law. They say that, by law, counties or cities cannot prevent police officers or sheriffs from telling federal agents that persons the police have arrested may be in the country illegally. As a White House statement from the spring of 2018 explained, "That means, according to Congress, a city that prohibits its officials from providing information to federal immigration authorities—a sanctuary city—is violating the law."[32]

The Trump administration has not tried to charge any officials in these cities with a crime. It has, however, threatened to penalize the cities in other ways. Immediately upon taking office, Trump signed an executive order that sought to withhold

"According to Congress, a city that prohibits its officials from providing information to federal immigration authorities—a sanctuary city—is violating the law."[32]

—A White House statement issued in the spring of 2018

Chicago's CityKey Program

Some sanctuary cities have moved aggressively to show their support for undocumented immigrants in their community. In April 2018 Chicago, Illinois, launched the CityKey card, a municipal identification (ID) card that was available to all Chicago residents, including those living in the country illegally. The card is a photo ID that does not include information about national origin or legal status. It is intended to serve as an official government-issued ID and can help the cardholder access city services. It can also be used as a library card and a fare card for public transit. By displaying the CityKey card, the user can get discounts at local businesses, museums, theaters, and concert halls. The card can even be used to file a police report or get married.

Critics of the program warned that undocumented immigrants could use the card to vote illegally. However, Rahm Emanuel, who was mayor when the program began, rejected these concerns. "Undocumented (people) cannot vote, and that's clear policy," he said at the launch event. "This is not about that. This is about accessing benefits." Undocumented immigrants worried that the information they provided to get the card would be kept on file at city hall, where it could be accessed by ICE officials and used to track down violators. City Clerk Anna Valencia assured immigrants that personal information about applicants would be destroyed before ICE agents could see it.

Quoted in John Byrne, "Emanuel Launches Municipal ID for Undocumented Immigrants, Others," *Chicago Tribune*, April 26, 2018. www.chicagotribune.com.

federal funds from sanctuary cities, but the move was blocked by the courts. Trump has also floated the idea of sending tens of thousands of newly arrived undocumented immigrants to sanctuary cities. "Last month alone, 100,000 illegal immigrants arrived at our borders, placing a massive strain on communities and schools and hospitals and public resources like nobody's ever seen before," Trump announced to a crowd of his supporters in Green Bay, Wisconsin, in April 2019. "Now we're sending many of them to sanctuary cities. Thank you very much. They're not too happy about it. I'm proud to tell you that was actually my sick idea."[33] Fact-checkers at the *Washington Post* and other outlets concluded that Trump's statements were untrue; even so, opponents of the president pledged to block such a move. Anonymous sources said Trump did pressure then-DHS secretary Kirstjen Nielsen to pursue the plan, but Nielsen resisted. Lawyers at the DHS decided the scheme likely was illegal.

A Push to Protect Immigrants and Refugees

The idea of sanctuary cities for undocumented immigrants goes back decades. It originated with religious groups. In the early 1980s poverty, violence, and civil war in Central America led waves of migrants and refugees to flee north to the United States. Church leaders were outraged when desperate people from Guatemala and El Salvador were turned away at the border or quickly deported if they somehow gained entry. They thought the federal government had a moral duty to accept the refugees and give them asylum in the United States.

A small group of clergy, led by the Reverend John Fife of the Southside Presbyterian Church of Tucson, Arizona, organized an underground network to smuggle refugees into the United States. Migrants would hide out in churches just across the US border, sometimes sleeping in the pews. Federal indictments of the faith leaders in 1985 for conspiracy and harboring undocumented immigrants were intended to stop the sanctuary movement. Instead, it swelled to include more than five hundred faith groups throughout the country. In addition, many cities adopted sanctuary policies and began calling themselves sanctuary cities. "You can't plan for a movement," Fife says of his influential acts of civil disobedience. "It just happened."[34]

In the ensuing years the federal government continued to remove huge numbers of undocumented immigrants each year. The INS, forerunner to ICE, worked to enlist local law enforcement in detaining and deporting these people. Police officers and sheriffs in small towns were asked to notify ICE any time they encountered a suspected "illegal." In return, local authorities received a federal detainer, or hold, allowing them to detain suspects for an additional forty-eight hours. This gave ICE agents enough time to swoop in, take custody of the undocumented immigrants, and prepare to deport them.

However, many local police departments chafed at this process. They disliked doing the work of federal immigration agents and they were uncomfortable about jailing undocumented immigrants for minor traffic violations or holding them without a warrant. They also believed that these immigrants were becoming reluctant to report crimes for fear of being detained. In 2014 a federal appeals court in Portland, Oregon, gave local police another reason to resist pressure from ICE. The court ruled that police in Oregon's Clackamas County had violated an immigrant woman's constitutional rights under the Fourth Amendment. The police had detained Maria Miranda-Olivares at the request of ICE agents even after her charges were settled and she was otherwise free to go. City officials and police departments across the nation now had legitimate concerns that honoring detainers from ICE could put them in jeopardy of being sued. Certain cities directed their police departments to no longer cooperate with federal immigration officials. With Trump's election and the start of more aggressive deportation efforts, additional cities and states joined the sanctuary movement. In a 2017 editorial, Portland mayor Ted Wheeler explained his own city's rationale for becoming a sanctuary city:

> We do not harbor criminals, but we will not aid in the deportation of our neighbors whose only offense is being undocumented. . . . Residents, regardless of immigration status, should not be afraid to go to the police with information on crimes for fear that they might be deported. They should not be afraid to access critical services or seek refuge from domestic abuse and homeless services. They should not be afraid to bring their children to school.[35]

The Kate Steinle Case

There is also strong opposition to cities and states declaring themselves as sanctuaries for undocumented immigrants. Early in Trump's presidency, the verdict in a controversial murder case brought new scrutiny to sanctuary cities. In 2015 thirty-two-year-old Kate Steinle was shot and killed while walking on a San Francisco pier with her father and a friend. Two years later Jose Ines Garcia Zarate, a homeless undocumented immigrant arraigned for Steinle's killing, was found not guilty of murder. The jury agreed with the defense position that the shooting was unintentional. (According to his attorneys, Garcia Zarate found a cloth-wrapped gun under his seat at the pier. When he picked it up, they said, it accidentally discharged. The bullet ricocheted off the ground and struck Steinle in the back.) In the same trial, Garcia Zarate was convicted on a lesser charge of illegally possessing a firearm—a conviction that was overturned by a California appeals court in August 2019.

Jose Ines Garcia Zarate (shown at right), an undocumented immigrant, was arrested in 2015 and later acquitted of murdering a young San Francisco woman. The controversial verdict led to renewed scrutiny of sanctuary cities.

Before the Steinle shooting, Garcia Zarate had been deported five times. As of August 2019, he was awaiting trial in federal prison on other charges. The Steinle case drew angry protests from those who favor tougher enforcement of immigration laws. They blamed Steinle's death on San Francisco's lax policies as a sanctuary city. Trump called Steinle's death a "senseless and totally preventable act of violence committed by an illegal immigrant."[36] Tom Homan, deputy director of ICE, said, "San

A "Welcoming City" in Trump Country

The term *sanctuary city* has become a political flash point during the Trump era. As a result, some cities intent on reaching out to their Hispanic residents call themselves "welcoming cities" instead. In July 2019 Oklahoma City, located in the heart of Trump country, hosted a meeting of the Oklahoma County Jail Trust to address concerns from immigrant rights activists. The activists complained that two ICE agents are permanently stationed at the county jail to assist with the booking process for inmates. This allows the agents to request a detainer on anyone whose name or fingerprints show up on a database of illegal immigrants. When such an inmate is released, it usually takes forty-eight hours for ICE agents to arrive and arrest the individual. And if the sheriff follows the welcoming city policy, he or she can refuse to honor the detainer request. But if ICE is already on-site, its agents can pick up the individual immediately without further assistance from the county.

Cynthia Garcia, who belongs to an organization for immigrant youth called United We Dream, wants the ICE agents removed from the county jail. She and other activists insist that local law enforcement should not be collaborating with Trump's deportation efforts. "I believe that funneling people into ICE and the deportation machine does not make us safer," Garcia told the jail trust members. "Families in Oklahoma do not feel safer with those two agents sitting in the Oklahoma County Jail." The trustees promised to listen and work out a new plan of action.

Quoted in Kayla Branch, "Jail Trust Meeting Focuses on Role of ICE," *Oklahoman* (Oklahoma City, OK), July 23, 2019. http://oklahoman.com.

Francisco's policy of refusing to honor ICE detainers is a blatant threat to public safety and undermines the rule of law."[37] High-profile conservatives in the media slammed the sanctuary city movement and helped gain passage of a new law in Congress, dubbed Kate's law, that increased penalties for criminal reentry into the United States.

In March 2019, as emotions were running high over immigration issues, the Steinle case once more made headlines. An appeals court dismissed a civil lawsuit by Steinle's parents claiming that negligence by the city of San Francisco had contributed to their daughter's death. The court ruled that under California law the officials could not be sued. According to the suit, the city's former sheriff had issued a memo in 2015 that forbade jail staff to notify ICE about undocumented immigrants. Garcia Zarate was released from custody in San Francisco even though ICE officials made a specific request to detain him. The Steinle lawsuit argued that the city's sanctuary policy was a direct violation of federal and state laws. Garcia Zarate will almost certainly be deported once again after the federal case concludes.

A National Divide on Sanctuary Cities

In response to the Steinle case and others, some states have taken steps to reject the sanctuary city movement. Florida is among at least twelve states that have passed laws to ban sanctuary cities. On June 16, 2019, Florida governor Ron DeSantis signed a bill that prohibits local governments from enacting policies designed to shield undocumented immigrants from being deported. The bill requires local police to honor ICE detainers for immigrants who are in custody or convicted of a crime. DeSantis signed the bill to cheers from supporters, some wearing the bright red Make America Great Again caps associated with Trump. "Sanctuary cities basically create law-free zones where people can come to our state illegally and our country illegally, commit criminal offenses and then just walk right out the door and continue to do it," said

DeSantis. "In Florida, that will not happen."[38] As part of the ceremony, DeSantis also introduced a Jacksonville man whose son had been killed by an undocumented driver with a history of two deportations.

At the same time, sanctuary cities around the nation have sought to do more on behalf of undocumented immigrants. Some cities provide interpreters and free legal advice to help undocumented people stay in the country. Some have programs to help pay for legal fees and even provide low-cost housing especially for undocumented immigrants. The legal website Nolo features the kind of advice that sanctuary cities offer to immigrants:

> It is important to realize that living in a sanctuary city provides no guarantees that you are safe from ICE detention and, ultimately, deportation. ICE is not barred from conducting operations in sanctuary cities. It often monitors the activities of suspected undocumented immigrants. Sweeps and arrests typically begin early in the morning, before people head to work or begin their day. Even though Houston, Austin, and Dallas are considered sanctuary cities, for example, it is not unusual to find ICE posted at bus stations coming from Mexico, or at grocery stores and construction sites or other establishments that typically cater to or employ Hispanics.[39]

Some communities pursue sanctuary protections for immigrants despite their location in states that reject such policies overall. For example, in Texas, sanctuary cities exist as islands in a surrounding sea of conservative opposition. California, which voted to become a sanctuary state, contains towns and jurisdictions that decline to follow the progressive line to protect the undocumented. Troy Edgar, the mayor of Los Alamitos in Or-

A woman in Miami, Florida, holds a sign in protest of the announcement that Miami would not function as a sanctuary city. Florida was one of the states that passed legislation against cities shielding undocumented immigrants from being deported.

ange County, wants his city to abide by federal law. "As a U.S. Navy veteran and a council member for 12 years," says Edgar, "I feel very strongly that this [state sanctuary law] is constitutionally wrong. I don't think this is an immigration issue. But I take issue with the state stepping in the middle."[40]

Sanctuary cities have risen in recent years to meet the challenge of Trump's tougher stance on illegal immigration. They are determined to thwart the deportation efforts of federal agencies such as ICE. However, polls show that Americans—including Hispanic Americans—overwhelmingly reject the idea of sanctuary cities. A 2018 Investor's Business Daily/TechnoMetrica poll found that 64 percent of Americans oppose the policy, while only 31 percent support it. Hispanics gave the policy a thumbs-down by a margin of 57 percent to 39 percent. Nonetheless, sanctuary cities and states refuse to back down from their beliefs. Despite the Trump administration's efforts to punish them, they welcome undocumented immigrants and seek to help them remain in the United States. Sanctuary cities continue to oppose Trump's immigration policies.

Chapter Five

A Search for Solutions at the Border

In June 2019, as caravans of migrants from Central America made their way toward the southern US border, Trump blamed the governments who failed to stop this exodus. He announced he was cutting off more than $550 million in aid to Honduras, Guatemala, and El Salvador to show his displeasure. As Trump explained, "We were paying them tremendous amounts of money, and we're not paying them anymore because they haven't done a thing for us."[41] A spokesperson for the US Department of State said the funds would not be restored until these governments took concrete action to reduce the number of migrants heading north to the United States. Migrants flee these countries to escape violent drug gangs and poverty in the so-called Northern Triangle of Central America. They view the United States as a place of safety and opportunity. Many hope to join friends and relatives who have managed to enter the United States. Trump's decision to withhold aid money seems unlikely to stanch the flow of immigrants. Opponents believe it will make things worse. But it also shows how the administration is struggling to find answers to the immigration crisis.

No Easy Solutions

Foreign policy analysts admit there are no easy solutions to the detention and deportation problem. But many consider Trump's attempts to blame other countries a misstep. "It's completely counterproductive," says Jason Marczak, an expert on Latin America policy at the Atlantic Council. "People leave those countries because of violence and lack of economic opportunity; US funding helps counter those dynamics."[42] Other analysts say aid helps reduce crime in Central America and provide better living conditions. They believe such aid should be increased, not withheld.

Democrats and many Republicans in Congress agree the cuts are a mistake. They regard it as cruel to withhold aid to countries where crime, violence, and hunger are widespread. "It's a really easy thing to say, 'Look they're sending migrants so just cut off their foreign aid,'" says Texas representative Mike McCaul, the highest-ranking Republican on the House Foreign Affairs Committee. "It's going to make things tragically worse."[43] Shortly after Trump's announcement, the House proposed a bill that would force the administration to make the aid payments, which Congress had already earmarked for Central America.

> "We were paying [Central American countries] tremendous amounts of money, and we're not paying them anymore because they haven't done a thing for us."[41]
>
> —President Donald Trump

Some are convinced that what the region needs is a huge new aid package going forward. Mexican president Andrés Manuel López Obrador has called for a $30 billion Central American Marshall Plan—the plan of economic aid that helped Europe rebuild after World War II. Some experts question whether aid money would do any good. They point out that governments in the Northern Triangle countries are riddled with corruption. The worry is that officials in these countries are more concerned about lining their pockets with American cash than using it to help their people. "The price of getting it wrong is steep—often more harmful than not sending aid at all," says Ryan C. Berg, a research fellow at the American Enterprise Institute. "In fact, poorly conceptualized foreign aid can stymie the deepening of democracy by propping up bad actors and providing them with an economic lifeline to mask their lack of success on reform."[44] In Berg's view, trying to stop the flow of migrants with a modern-day Marshall Plan would likely be another futile gesture.

A Push for Tougher Enforcement

The debate over detention and deportation of undocumented immigrants has become a bitter standoff, with little room for compromise. Progressives and conservatives in America fundamentally disagree on how to solve the crisis at the border. Conservatives remain opposed to lax enforcement of immigration laws. Most agree with Trump's tweet of June 19, 2018: "If you don't have Borders, you don't have a Country!"[45] They want tougher policies overall on detention and deportation. Generally, they support Trump's efforts to deter illegal immigrants by promising to arrest them and deport them as quickly as possible. Conservatives believe that providing illegal immigrants with a pathway to citizenship rewards them for breaking the law and encourages more migrants to enter the country illegally. Conservatives support asylum for refugees who are legitimately fleeing violence or oppression. However, they argue that many of the migrants who apply for asylum do not actually qualify but are actually seeking jobs and better lives, which their own countries cannot provide.

The huge number of migrants seeking asylum, whether or not they have a legitimate case, has strained resources. To deal with overcrowding in detention centers, conservatives want to increase funding for ICE. Since ICE is primarily responsible for detention of migrants, that would allow the agency to hold individuals and families in clean housing with plenty of space until they can be processed. Many conservatives note that the border patrol also supports more funding for ICE. "Now why doesn't ICE have funding?" asked Republican Senator James Lankford of Oklahoma after a fact-finding trip to the border. "Because it's been one of our biggest battles with our Democratic colleagues that are obsessed with defunding ICE. Over and over again they say they want to

A large group of Central American migrants walk along a road in Mexico hoping to cross into the United States. President Trump has blamed the governments of Honduras, Guatemala, and El Salvador for failing to stop the exodus of migrants.

abolish ICE, defund ICE, get rid of ICE. What's really being stated [is] there's no place to do detention when that occurs."[46]

Conservatives would do away with the twenty-day release rule under the Flores agreement. They claim this time limit does not allow for proper processing of migrants before they must be released and can then disappear into the population. Many conservatives also want to hire more ICE attorneys, asylum officers, and immigration judges and station them closer to the border. They believe this would lead to much more efficient processing of asylum seekers and other migrants. "Nobody's going to get elected saying 'I'm going to solve the border crisis by hiring a lot of immigration judges,' but the simple reality is . . . hire more immigration judges," says John Sandweg,

"Now why doesn't ICE have funding? Because it's been one of our biggest battles with our Democratic colleagues that are obsessed with defunding ICE."[46]

—Republican senator James Lankford of Oklahoma

former acting director of ICE. "You can have speed without detention centers, you just need to hire double, triple the size of the immigration court."[47] Despite these recommendations, Trump has opposed the idea of hiring more immigration judges.

More Lenient Approaches

One result of Trump's policies has been to bring progressives together on the issue of immigration. "Trump in a weird way unified us," says Jorge L. Barón of the Northwest Immigrant Rights Project. "Whatever divisions there used to be, his attacks have

---

Trump's "Third-Country" Rule for Asylum

To relieve overcrowded detention centers at the US border, the Trump administration has sought to reduce the number of migrants seeking asylum at the border. One plan is the so-called third-country rule. This tough new asylum rule requires migrants who travel through a third country on their way to the United States to apply for refugee status in that country first, instead of at the US border. Failure to follow this procedure leaves a migrant ineligible for asylum. DHS acting secretary Kevin K. McAleenan says the rule would help reduce the incentives for migration to the United States until Congress could act to ease the border crisis.

Opposition from immigrant rights groups, including the ACLU, was swift. Opponents of the new rule said it only increased burdens on refugees who were already desperate to find a secure situation. They also contended that the rule would not work unless the United States had a prior agreement with the so-called third countries. On July 24, 2019, these concerns were echoed by a federal court in San Francisco that temporarily blocked the new rule. US district court judge Jon Tigar noted that the countries' migrants must cross to reach the US border are hardly safe havens. As Tigar declared at the hearing, "The administrative record about the dangers faced by persons transiting through Mexico and the inadequacy of the asylum system there . . . is stunning." Tigar's ruling put the new plan on hold while other courts were reviewing whether it is constitutional.

Quoted in Daniel Trotta and Kristina Cooke, "U.S. Judge Blocks Trump's Latest Sweeping Asylum Rule," *Reuters*, July 24, 2019. www.reuters.com.

---

gone through so many people that all of us feel embattled."[48] After years of inaction on border issues, progressives today are debating more lenient approaches to the detention and deportation crisis. They refer to those who seek entry at the US border as "our neighbors." They favor a path to citizenship for the undocumented, especially those who have been in the United States for years and have put down roots. Progressives want policies that enable migrant family members and relatives to reunite in the United States. They also support Deferred Action for Childhood Arrivals (DACA) and other programs that allow those who came to the country unlawfully to remain and get work permits.

Progressives insist that the United States has a moral duty to accept refugees at the border who are legitimately seeking asylum from violence, persecution, and poverty in their own countries. Many see an urgent need to uphold the asylum system, which they fear Trump is trying to dismantle. Michael Posner, director of the Center for Business and Human Rights, says:

> The United States is a nation founded by immigrants, many of whom were themselves refugees fleeing religious persecution. It also is a country that was built on a legal framework, rooted in the Constitution, which established due process of law as a central tenet. The abandonment of a law-based approach to refugee protection betrays this history and flies in the face of our rule-of-law tradition.[49]

Reports on conditions at detention facilities have outraged progressives across the nation. They want the Flores agreement strictly enforced to ensure that detention centers are safe and sanitary. To relieve overcrowding, progressives would release detainees into the community much more promptly while the detainees await their hearings. Warnings about immigrant crime and violence strike progressives as deceptive and overblown.

Some progressives favor an even more lenient approach to migrant rights and border security. They believe in amnesty for the undocumented. This would allow those living in the country illegally to remain without further penalty and even become citizens. Growing numbers of progressives say they support something close to open borders. At a Democratic presidential debate in June 2019, all ten candidates favored reducing the offense of illegally crossing the border to the equivalent of a parking ticket. Many progressives also want to abolish ICE altogether. They believe that funding for ICE inevitably means building more detention centers, which to them only bolsters Trump's aggressive efforts to arrest undocumented immigrants. With such a huge divide in their views, it is no surprise that American progressives and conservatives are struggling to find areas of compromise on immigration.

The Remain-in-Mexico Program

One controversial Trump administration program has shown some success in reducing the flow of migrants across the border. The Migrant Protection Protocols (MPP)—also called "Remain in Mexico"—diverts asylum-seeking migrants back to border cities in northern Mexico, such as Juárez and Tijuana. There they are detained in shelters while they await a final decision from US immigration courts. From April to July 2019, more than eight thousand migrants were transported back to Mexican cities. US officials hoped the new policy, launched in cooperation with Mexico, would lead many potential migrants to reconsider the long journey north in the future.

However, critics say the MPP program is putting migrants' lives in danger. The cities in northern Mexico where they are sent are hotbeds of drug violence. Juárez has seen five murders a day on average since April 2019. Migrants who returned to the US immigration court in El Paso, Texas, have shared harrowing sto-

A migrant woman helps her son with his jacket inside a shelter in Tijuana, Mexico. After fleeing violence in El Salvador and seeking asylum in the United States, she was ordered back to Tijuana under the Trump administration's "Remain in Mexico" policy.

ries of robbery, kidnapping, and sexual assault while in Mexico. "There are many human rights violations—too many," says Javier Calvillo, a priest who runs the largest migrant shelter in Juárez. "No plan, even if it involves the government, churches and private business, can succeed if we continue to have deaths, kidnappings, human traffickers and if people don't respect the rights of migrants."[50] News reports also claim that migrants in the MPP program have little chance of success on their asylum claims. Only about 1 percent of those held in Mexico have later been allowed into the United States to pursue their bids.

"No plan, even if it involves the government, churches and private business, can succeed if we continue to have deaths, kidnappings, human traffickers and if people don't respect the rights of migrants."[50]

—Javier Calvillo, a priest who runs the largest migrant shelter in Juárez, Mexico

Expanding Work Permits for Foreign Workers

Trump has repeatedly declared that the United States is full, with no room for more immigrants at the southern border. Yet in April 2019 the federal government announced a plan to issue more work permits for foreign workers from Mexico and other Latin American countries. In a joint statement from the DHS and the US Department of Labor, the government said it was ready to issue as many as thirty thousand additional H-2B visas for workers through September 30, 2019, which is the end of the fiscal year. Usually Congress caps the number of visas at sixty-six thousand. However, with the American economy doing well, more businesses have seasonal jobs available. These include jobs in restaurants, hotels, landscaping, farms, and construction.

Experts have suggested that expanding temporary work permits for migrant workers could help ease the chaos at the border. The administration already claims that many asylum seekers are actually in search of jobs. Alex Nowrasteh, a senior immigration analyst with the Cato Institute, sees major contradictions in the government's policy on visiting workers. "On one hand, we need more people because the economy is booming," he says. "Then on the other hand, to say, 'The country is full, go back'— it's impossible to reconcile those."

Quoted in Mihir Zaveri and Emily S. Rueb, "U.S. Wants to Allow More Foreign Workers While Also Restricting Immigration," *New York Times*, April 8, 2019. www.nytimes.com.

Electronic Surveillance for Detainees

Another way to reduce populations in US detention facilities is to use alternatives to detention, or ATDs. One ATD is electronic surveillance for detainees. ICE employs thousands of electronic monitoring devices, or ankle monitors, to keep track of immigrants on release. These monitors have proved to be humane and economical, if not entirely effective. The lightweight devices, which weigh 5.5 ounces (156 g) each, allow immigrants who are considered low risk for escape or violence to be released into the community. The result is more space for immigrants who are required to remain in detention. With an ankle monitor, an immigrant can be tracked and supervised by immigration authorities while awaiting his or her court proceeding. Savings from the use of monitors is enormous. Detention in an immigrant center costs more than $200 a day per individual, while the use of ankle monitors costs only about $20 a day.

The monitors are not without drawbacks. For one thing, they are far from tamperproof. ICE claims that about three in ten immigrants with ankle monitors cut them off and ditch them before their hearings. The monitors are also restrictive. Each monitor must be recharged about every six hours, so the wearer must maintain access to a power outlet. Immigrants from Central America call them *grilletes*, meaning "shackles." They claim that the monitors are uncomfortable, cause swelling, and restrict movement. Immigrants also regard them as a source of shame in the community. "When you go out into the street, the whole world stops to look at your feet,"[51] says one Honduran woman.

An immigrant from Honduras is shown wearing an ankle monitor as he waits at a Catholic Charities facility in San Antonio, Texas. These monitors allow immigration authorities to track and supervise immigrants who are awaiting court hearings.

Another ATD involves assigning a caseworker to make periodic checks on a migrant's whereabouts and situation. A caseworker can also help migrants navigate the process of immigration court. A third ATD sets a monetary incentive, or bond, to ensure that the migrant shows up for a hearing. Some ICE offices use all three of these ATD methods at once.

The search for solutions to the crisis over detentions and deportations has produced few examples of success. The Trump administration has tried to punish the Central American countries that refugees and asylum seekers are fleeing by cutting off aid. But critics warn that such cuts are likely to make matters worse in those countries. Trump's MPP policy has reduced the number of detainees in the United States by holding them in Mexican cities. But the result has been threats to the safety of these migrants, with no improvement in the asylum process. With conservatives and progressives bitterly divided on immigration issues, solutions to the detention crisis remain elusive.

Introduction: An Ongoing Immigration Crisis

1. Quoted in John Burnett, "'Thank God We're OK.' Migrants Tell of Conditions in a Texas Holding Facility," NPR, May 23, 2019. www.npr.org.
2. Quoted in Brent D. Griffiths, "Trump: 'We Cannot Allow All of These People to Invade Our Country,'" *Politico*, June 24, 2018. www.politico.com.
3. Quoted in Caitlin Dickerson, "Border at 'Breaking Point' as More than 76,000 Unauthorized Migrants Cross in a Month," *New York Times*, March 5, 2019. www.nytimes.com.

Chapter One: Family Separations at the Border

4. Quoted in Miriam Jordan, "'It's Horrendous': The Heartache of a Migrant Boy Taken from His Father," *New York Times*, June 7, 2018. www.nytimes.com.
5. Quoted in Jordan, "'It's Horrendous.'"
6. Quoted in Lisa Riordan Seville and Hannah Rappleye, "Trump Admin Ran 'Pilot Program' for Separating Migrant Families in 2017," NBC News, June 29, 2018. www.nbcnews.com.
7. Quoted in Maya Rhodan, "Here Are the Facts About President Trump's Family Separation Policy," *Time*, June 18, 2018. www.time.com.
8. Quoted in Nathaniel Weixel, "Agencies Were Surprised at Trump 'Zero Tolerance' Border Policy, Report Finds," *The Hill* (Washington, DC), October 24, 2018. www.thehill.com.
9. Quoted in Michael D. Shear et al., "Trump Retreats on Separating Families, but Thousands May Remain Apart," *New York Times*, June 20, 2018. www.nytimes.com.
10. Quoted in Laura Barrón-López, "Democrats Vow to Keep Fighting Trump's 'Zero Tolerance' Immigration Policy," *Washington Examiner*, June 21, 2018. www.washingtonexaminer.com.
11. Nicholas Wu, "What Is the Flores Agreement, and What Happens If the Trump Administration Withdraws from It?," Just Security, October 18, 2018. www.justsecurity.org.
12. Quoted in Alan Gomez, "Judge May Force Trump Administration to Reunite Thousands More Separated Families," *USA Today*, February 22, 2019. www.usatoday.com.

Chapter Two: Health and Safety Issues at Detention Centers

13. Quoted in Joel Rose and John Burnett, "DHS Inspector General Finds 'Dangerous Overcrowding' in Border Patrol Facilities," NPR, July 2, 2019. www.npr.org.

14. Quoted in Sarah Ferris, "Dems Seize Offensive Against Trump After Detention Center Outrage," *Politico*, July 3, 2019. www.politico.com.

15. Quoted in Jamey Keaten, "United Nations Slams US for Detention Facilities: 'This Should Never Happen Anywhere,'" *USA Today*, July 8, 2019. www.usatoday.com.

16. Quoted in Michael Collins and David Jackson, "Trump Says Detention Facilities 'Beautifully Run' After Report Describes Dangerous Conditions," *USA Today*, July 5, 2019. www.usatoday.com.

17. Quoted in Zoë Carpenter, "Democrats Confront the Horror at the Border," *The Nation*, June 26, 2019. www.thenation.com.

18. Quoted in Christina Zhao, "GOP Senator Rips Ocasio-Cortez for Calling Detention Centers 'Concentration Camps': 'Voices in Her Head Are Not Real,'" *Newsweek*, July 3, 2019. www.newsweekcom.

19. Lyndon Haviland, "Nielsen Resignation Doesn't Change Fact Child Sexual Abuse at Border Is Real Emergency," *USA Today*, April 9, 2019. www.usatoday.com.

20. Quoted in Graham Kates, "'I'm Hungry Here at Clint All the Time': Lawyers Use Kids' Testimonies to Seek Access to Border Patrol Facilities," CBS News, June 27, 2019. www.cbsnews.com.

21. Quoted in Simon Romero et al., "The Stuff of Nightmares: Inside the Migrant Detention Center in Clint, Texas," *USA Today*, July 7, 2019. www.usatoday.com.

Chapter Three: Aggressive Deportation Efforts

22. Quoted in Alan Neuhauser, "Trump Tweets of ICE Plan to Potentially Deport 'Millions,'" *U.S. News & World Report*, June 18, 2019. www.usnews.com.

23. Quoted in Ferris, "Dems Seize Offensive Against Trump After Detention Center Outrage."

24. Quoted in Colin Campbell, "'People Are Really, Really Afraid': Mass-Deportation Threat Strikes Fear into Baltimore Immigrants," *Baltimore Sun*, June 24, 2019. www.baltimoresun.com.

25. Quoted in Franco Ordoñez and Bobby Allyn, "Trump Delays Immigration Raids, Giving Democrats 'Two Weeks' to Change Asylum Laws," NPR, June 22, 2019. www.npr.org.
26. Quoted in Ronn Blitzer, "Vintage Clip Shows Obama Warning Migrant Families: 'Do Not Send Your Children,'" Fox News, June 27, 2019. www.foxnews.com.
27. Quoted in Zachary B. Wolf, "Yes, Obama Deported More People than Trump but Context Is Everything," CNN, July 13, 2019. www.cnn.com.
28. Quoted in Wolf, "Yes, Obama Deported More People than Trump but Context Is Everything."
29. Quoted in Dara Lind, "Donald Trump Promises to Deport 3 Million 'Illegal Immigrant Criminals.' That's Literally Impossible," Vox, November 14, 2016. www.vox.com.
30. Quoted in Massoud Hayoun, "The Trump Administration's Plan to Reduce the Immigration Court Backlog Will Only Add to It," *Pacific Standard*, April 18, 2019. www.psmag.com.

Chapter Four: The Rise of Sanctuary Cities

31. Quoted in Roz Plater, "Hundreds Turn Out for Berkeley ICE Protest," NBC Bay Area, July 13, 2019. www.nbcbayarea.com.
32. Quoted in Deirdre Shesgreen and Alan Gomez, "Sanctuary Cities for Illegal Immigrants? Here's What You Need to Know," *USA Today*, April 12, 2019. www.usatoday.com.
33. Quoted in Justin Wise, "Trump Says US Is Sending Immigrants to Sanctuary Cities: 'That Was My Sick Idea,'" *Hill* (Washington, DC), April 28, 2019. www.thehill.com.
34. Quoted in Amanda Sakuma, "No Safe Place," MSNBC, 2019. www.msnbc.com.
35. Ted Wheeler, "'Sanctuary City' Means Portland Will Remain Welcoming to All," *Oregonian* (Portland, OR), January 29, 2017. www.oregonlive.com.
36. Quoted in Christina Maxouris, "Kate Steinle's Parents Can't Sue 'Sanctuary City' for Failing to Tell ICE About Shooter's Release," CNN, March 26, 2019. www.cnn.com.
37. Quoted in Maxouris, "Kate Steinle's Parents Can't Sue 'Sanctuary City' for Failing to Tell ICE About Shooter's Release."
38. Associated Press, "Advocates Say Florida Governor's 'Sanctuary Bill' Politically Motivated," NBC News, June 16, 2019. www.nbcnews.com.
39. Nolo, "As an Undocumented Immigrant, Am I Safer from Deportation in a Sanctuary City?," 2019. www.nolo.com.

40. Quoted in Tatiana Sanchez, "California Cities Are Rebelling Against State Sanctuary Law, but How Far Can They Go?," *San Jose (CA) Mercury News*, April 23, 2018. www.mercury news.com.

Chapter Five: A Search for Solutions at the Border

41. Quoted in Ted Hesson, "Democrats Fume as Trump Cuts Central American Aid," *Politico*, March 31, 2019. www.po litico.com.
42. Quoted in Demetri Sevastopulo et al., "Donald Trump Cuts Off Aid to Three Central American States," *Financial Times* (London), June 17, 2019. www.ft.com.
43. Quoted in Andrea Drusch, "Trump Wants to Halt Aid to Central America. These Republicans Want to Stop Him," *Fort Worth (TX) Star-Telegram*, April 1, 2019. www.star-telegram.com.
44. Ryan C. Berg, "A Central American Marshall Plan Won't Work," *Foreign Policy*, March 5, 2019. www.foreignpolicy.com.
45. Donald J. Trump (@realDonaldTrump), "If you don't have Borders, you don't have a Country!," Twitter, June 19, 2018. https://twitter.com.
46. James Lankford, "Senator Lankford Stresses Support for Border Agents After Trip to US-Mexico Border," James Lankford, United States Senator for Oklahoma, July 24, 2019. www .lankford.senate.gov.
47. Quoted in Tess Bonn, "Former ICE Chief: Hire More Immigration Judges," *Hill* (Washington, DC), August 1, 2018. www .thehill.com.
48. Quoted in Robert Draper, "The Democrats Have an Immigration Problem," *New York Times*, October 10, 2018. www .nytimes.com.
49. Michael Posner, "U.S. Should Not Abandon Leadership on Asylum," *Forbes*, November 9, 2018. www.forbes.com.
50. Quoted in Robert Moore, "In Juárez, 'Remain in Mexico' Policy Casts Asylum-Seekers Back into Uncertainty," NPR, July 10, 2019. www.npr.org.
51. Quoted in Kyle Barron and Cinthya Santos Briones, "No Alternative: Ankle Monitors Expand the Reach of Immigration Detention," NACLA, January 6, 2015. www.nacla.org.

American Civil Liberties Union (ACLU)—www.aclu.org

The ACLU works in the courts, legislatures, and communities to preserve and defend the individual rights and liberties that the US Constitution guarantees to all people. The ACLU's Immigrants' Rights Project addresses immigration issues that include workplace rights, detention and deportation, and discrimination.

Center for Immigration Studies (CIS)—www.cis.org

The CIS is an independent, nonprofit research organization that publishes a variety of reports and articles that examine the social, economic, environmental, security, and economic consequences of both legal and illegal immigration. The CIS believes that debates informed by objective data will lead to better immigration policies.

Federation for American Immigration Reform (FAIR)—
www.fairus.org

FAIR is a national nonprofit organization of citizens who share the belief that America's immigration policies must be reformed to serve the national interest. FAIR seeks to stop all illegal immigration, favors greatly enhanced border security, and supports policies that would lower legal immigration levels.

Heritage Foundation—www.heritage.org

Founded in 1973, the Heritage Foundation is a research and educational institution that seeks to formulate and promote conservative public policies. It supports immigration policies that protect immigrants who enter the United States through legal channels and advocates sharp measures to deter illegal immigration.

Migration Policy Institute—www.migrationpolicy.org

This nonpartisan institute conducts authoritative research and publishes the online journal *Migration Information Source* with the goal of improving immigration policy through learning and dialogue. The institute has offices in the United States and Europe to provide a global perspective to immigration issues.

National Immigration Forum—www.immigrationforum.org

The National Immigration Forum advocates for the rights of all immigrants and promotes federal immigration policies that embrace America's tradition as a nation of immigrants. The forum publishes and distributes a wide range of educational materials, including fact sheets, issue papers, and other reading materials.

US Citizenship and Immigration Services (USCIS)—
www.uscis.gov

A branch of the DHS, the USCIS oversees lawful immigration in the United States. This includes granting all immigration and citizenship benefits and setting policies regarding who will be allowed to enter the United States. Its website provides information on current immigration laws and regulations.

Books

Beth C. Caldwell, *Deported Americans: Life After Deportation to Mexico*. Durham, NC: Duke University Press, 2019.

Julie Hirschfeld Davis and Michael D. Shear, *Border Wars: Inside Trump's Assault on Immigration*. New York: Simon & Schuster, 2019.

Melvin Delgado, *Sanctuary Cities, Communities, and Organizations: A Nation at a Crossroads*. New York: Oxford University Press, 2018.

Stuart A. Kallen, *Crisis on the Border: Refugees and Undocumented Immigrations*. San Diego, CA: ReferencePoint, 2020.

Matthew Soerens and Jenny Yang, *Welcoming the Stranger: Justice, Compassion & Truth in the Immigration Debate*. Westmont, IL: InterVarsity, 2018.

Bob Woodward, *Fear: Trump in the White House*. New York: Simon & Schuster, 2018.

Internet Sources

Ted Hesson, "Here's What's Driving the 'Crisis' at the Border," *Politico*, March 28, 2019. www.politico.com.

Miriam Jordan, "More than 2,000 Migrants Were Targeted in Raids. 35 Were Arrested," *New York Times*, July 23, 2019. www.nytimes.com.

Amanda Sakuma, "No Safe Place," MSNBC. www.msnbc.com.

Adam Serwer, "A Crime by Any Name," *Atlantic*, July 3, 2019. www.theatlantic.com.

Catherine E. Shoichet et al., "Inside America's Hidden Border," CNN, 2018. www.cnn.com.

John Allen is a writer who lives in Oklahoma City.